The Donkey And The King

(A Story of Redemption)

Lorilyn Roberts

Illustrated by Linda S. DiFranco

THE DONKEY AND THE KING

Lorilyn Roberts
Illustrated by Linda S. DiFranco

TO
MANISHA HOPE
AND
JOYLIN

As you look at the illustrations, remember that "good" can be found everywhere.

Bible quote on page 32 taken from the NIV Study Bible, ©1985, the Zondervan Corporation.

"The Donkey and the King" by Lorilyn Roberts. ISBN 1-58939-518-2.

Published 2004 by Virtualbookworm.com Publishing Inc., P.O. Box 9949, College Station, TX, 77842, US.

Manufactured in the United States of America.

Darkness fell on the stable and clouds cast shadows over the wilderness. Baruch twitched his ears and opened the gate.

"Do I want to spend the rest of my life as a beast of burden?" Baruch murmured. "I'm tired of carrying around things I don't want to carry."

Worldly Crow squawked, "You're making a big mistake. I know because I've been around. You're headed for trouble."

Much Afraid, a brown and white crippled dog, followed close behind.

"Please don't go," she cried.

"I'll miss you," grunted Lowly the pig, "and all the fun times we had together."

Baruch thought about how different things would be beyond the gate. No one to tell him what to do and no more chores!

"I have to go," said the donkey. "Someday I'll come back and we can be together again."

Baruch slipped away into the darkness.

$\mathscr{S}$everal hours passed as Baruch plodded along the unfamiliar road. Night winds blew dust in his face. Bats circled in the moonlit sky. Wild jackals H-O-W-L-E-D.

The moon cast dark shadows all around Baruch. Hungry lions
R-O-A-R-E-D in the distance.

The donkey found a cold, dark cave to sleep in, but
there was no soft hay for his bed.
"I miss my friends," he said, as he plopped down
on the hard ground.

Tears fell from Baruch's face and made puddles in the sand. He shivered from the cold and tried to cover his legs with his warm neck.

Out of nowhere, a white sheep poked her head
around the corner.
"Can I help you? It looks like you need a friend."

"My name is Baruch and I'm lost."

"I can see that," said the sheep. "My name is Little.

I was sent to find you."

"To find me?" Baruch asked. "You don't even know me."

"That's true," said Little. "But the King knows you."

"The King? He knows me?"

"That's right," said the sheep.

"Oh, no," cried Baruch. "The King must know I ran away.

He'll punish me and send me back, or worse, beat me!"

The donkey became very afraid. He didn't know what to do.

"You say that because you don't know the King. Come with
me, and I'll take you to him. You can't stay here.
It's too cold and dangerous."
Baruch knew she was right. "All right," he said.
"But I'm very scared."

The donkey and the sheep took off down the road.
"We are going to a garden," said the sheep. "It's a beautiful place full
of flowers, friends, and, most of all, the King, but..."
"But what?" Baruch asked.

"There is only one gate, one door, one place to get in.

An angel guards it with a flaming sword.

You must hear the King's voice to enter the garden."

*B*aruch didn't know what to think.

He had run away from home.

"I'm not a very good donkey," he said.

"I don't think I could hear the King's voice. He wouldn't want me. Maybe I shouldn't come with you."

The sheep said, "The King sent me to you, remember?

You were lost and lonely, but the King found you."

*L*ittle told many stories to Baruch about the King. Though

many hours passed it seemed but a few.

Baruch began to see himself not as a beast of burden,

but as a donkey that the King loved.

Soon they came upon the King's garden.

An angel with a flaming sword stood guard.

The donkey's heart pounded as he approached.

"I hope I can hear the King's voice," said Baruch.

Stillness filled the air. The circling bats had flown away.
No longer could Baruch hear the roaring of lions
or the howling of jackals. The donkey treasured in his heart
all the things the sheep had told him about the King.
Baruch closed his eyes and longed to meet Him.

Baruch walked toward the flaming sword.

He heard the King call his name "Baruch."

"I am not afraid," he said. "I know the King loves me."

Tears of joy fell from his face and covered the flames.

The donkey walked through the gate.

$\mathscr{B}$eautiful singing filled Baruch's ears.

"Welcome to the King's garden," the white dove cooed.

"Let me kiss your tired feet," the white dog cried.

"The King is coming," said the pig. "Look!"

The King stood before the donkey as strong as a mighty warrior,

but as gentle as a lamb.

He placed His hand on the donkey's head.

"I love you," the King said.

How could it have taken Baruch so long to find the King? But the King had found him. The sheep that had brought him to the garden had left, but maybe he would see her again.

The King smiled warmly at Baruch, "You were lost, but now you are found."

Come to me, all you who are weary and burdened, and I will give you rest. Take my yoke upon you and learn from me, for I am gentle and humble in heart, and you will find rest for your souls. For my yoke is easy and my burden is light.

Matthew 11:28-30